THIS BOOK BELONGS TO: -

SHIP'S CAPTAIN :

_____

FIREBOAT

A Fireboat is specialized with pumps and nozzles designed for fighting shoreline and shipboard fires. Fireboats have an effectively unlimited supply of water available, pumping water directly from below the hull. Fireboats can be used to assist shore-based firefighters when other water is in low supply. Some modern fireboats are capable of pumping tens of thousands of gallons of water per minute. Fireboats may also carry rescue workers. Passengers from ships in danger can be also transferred to various kind of rescue boats. Cities with fireboats are usually located on a large body of water with port facilities.

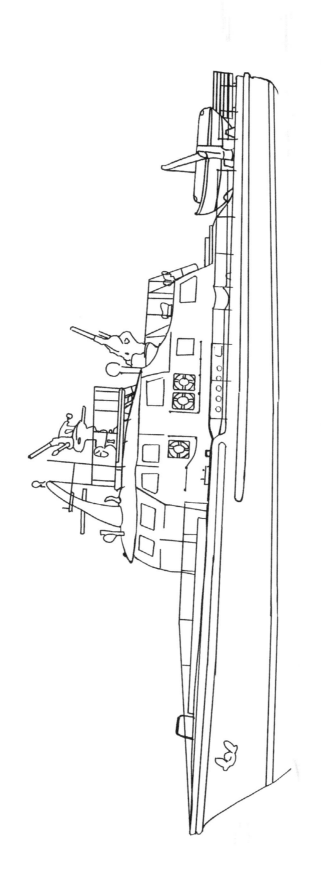

DAWB – Deep Ocean Work Boat

Deep Ocean Work Boats are used for many purposes from building off shore wind farms to laying underwater cables. They also support off shore drilling platforms and maintenance of lighthouses and navigation aids such as buoys and channel markers.

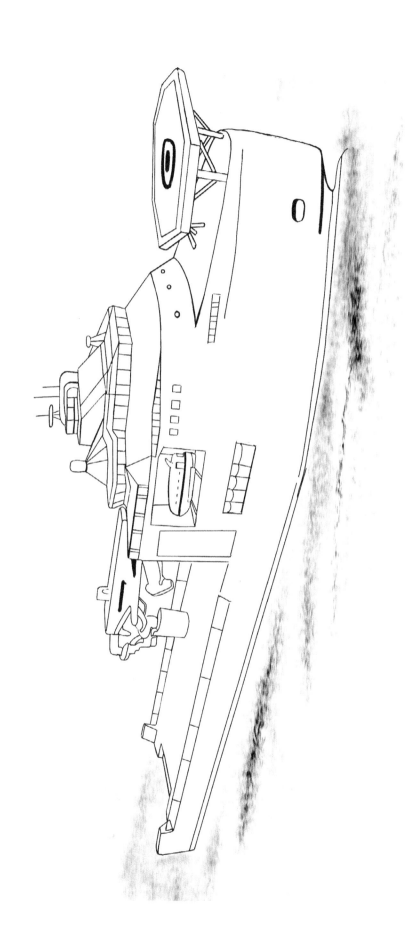

LIFEBOAT

Ship-launched lifeboats are lowered from davits or launched from a ship's deck They are very hard to sink and can withstand rough seas. The hard shell serves as protection from sun, wind, waves and rain. Lifeboats have flares and mirrors for signaling, first aid supplies and food and water for several days. Some lifeboats like the one pictured are equipped to permit self-rescue, with a radio, an engine and sail, heater, navigational equipment, solar water stills, rainwater catchments and fishing equipment. The International Convention for the Safety of Life at Sea (SOLAS) and the International Life-Saving Appliance Code (LSA) require certain emergency equipment on each lifeboat. Modern lifeboats carry an Emergency Position-Indicating Radio Beacon (EPIRB) and a radar reflector a Search and Rescue Transponder (SART) or both.

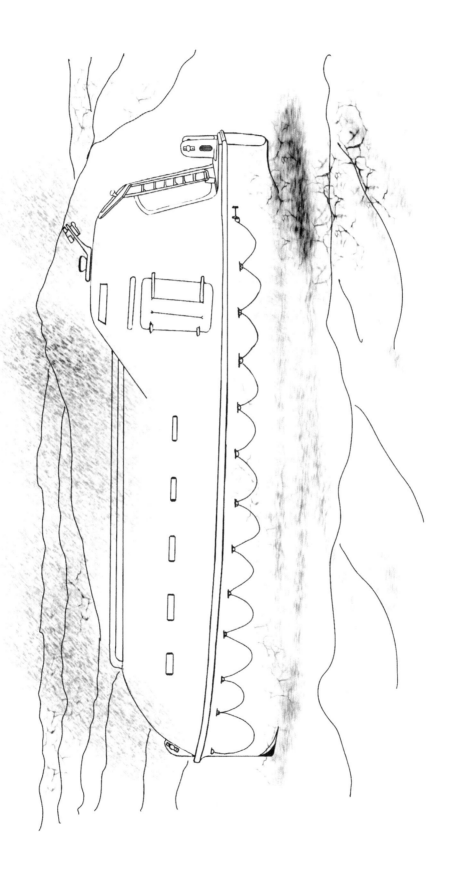

CATAMARAN

A Catamaran or 'Cat.' is a multi-hulled watercraft featuring two hulls of equal size. They are geometry-stabilized craft with a wide beam, rather than a heavy keel like a monohulled sailboat. Catamarans range in size from small sailing or rowing vessels to large naval ships. The structure connecting a catamaran's two hulls ranges from a simple frame strung with webbing to support the crew to a bridging superstructure incorporating extensive cabin and/or cargo space such as the one pictured.

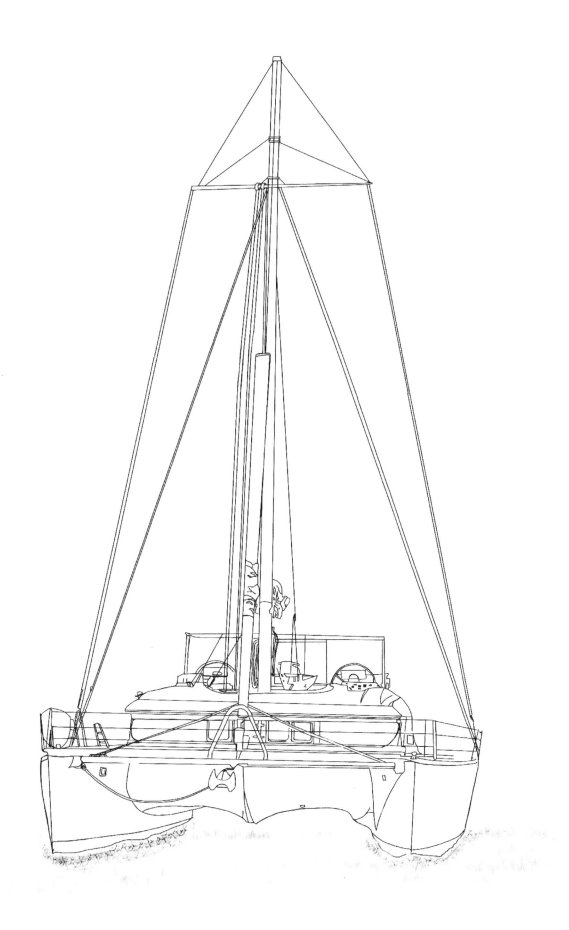

AIRCRAFT CARRIER

An Aircraft Carrier serves as a navy's seagoing airbase. Modern navies use several variants of the type. These variants are sometimes categorized as sub-types of aircraft carriers such as assault ships, fleet carriers and supercarriers. As of September 2017, there are 41 active aircraft carriers in the world operated by thirteen navies. The United States Navy has 11 large nuclear-powered supercarriers, carrying up to around 80 fighter jets each.

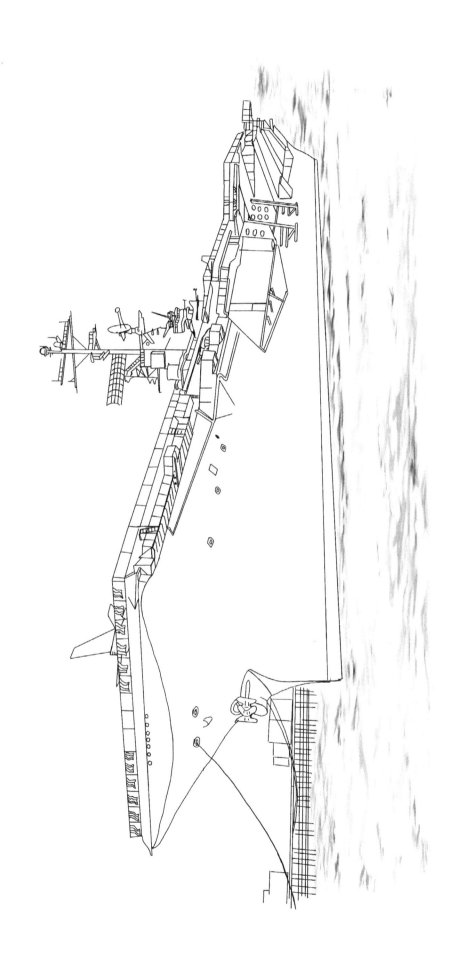

VIKING WARSHIP

The Viking Warship was perhaps the greatest technical and artistic achievement of the European dark ages. They were fast ships and had the strength to survive ocean crossings. These ships were an important part of Viking society, not only as a means of transportation, but also for the prestige that it conferred on her owner and skipper. Their ships permitted the Vikings to embark on their voyages of trading, of raiding, and of exploration. The crew's shields were arrayed along the gunwales, held in place by a shield rack to keep them out of the way.

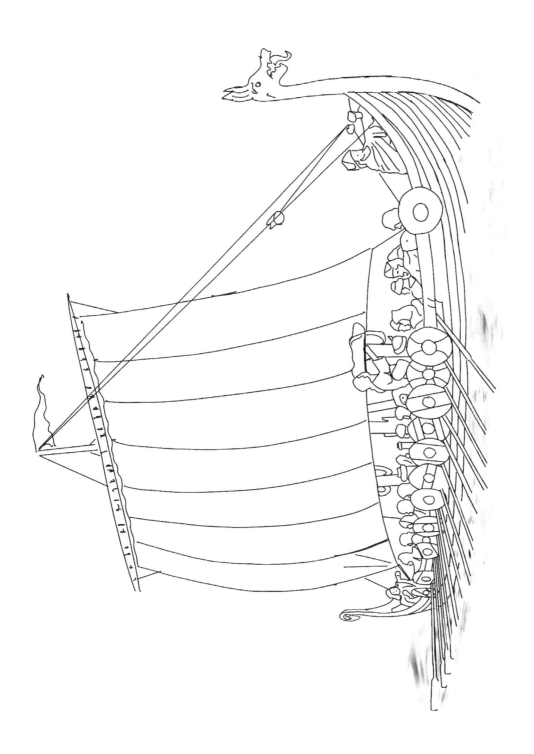

CRUISE SHIP

A Cruise Ship or Cruise Liner is a passenger ship used for pleasure voyages, where the voyage itself and the ship's amenities are a part of the experience, particularly on cruises that return passengers to their originating port. By contrast, dedicated transport oriented ocean liners transport passengers from one port to another. rather than on round trips. The gradual evolution of passenger ship design from ocean liners to cruise ships has seen passenger cabins shifted from inside the hull to the superstructure with private verandas. Modern cruise ships, have added amenities to cater to tourists, and recent vessels have been described as "balcony-laden floating luxury condominiums.

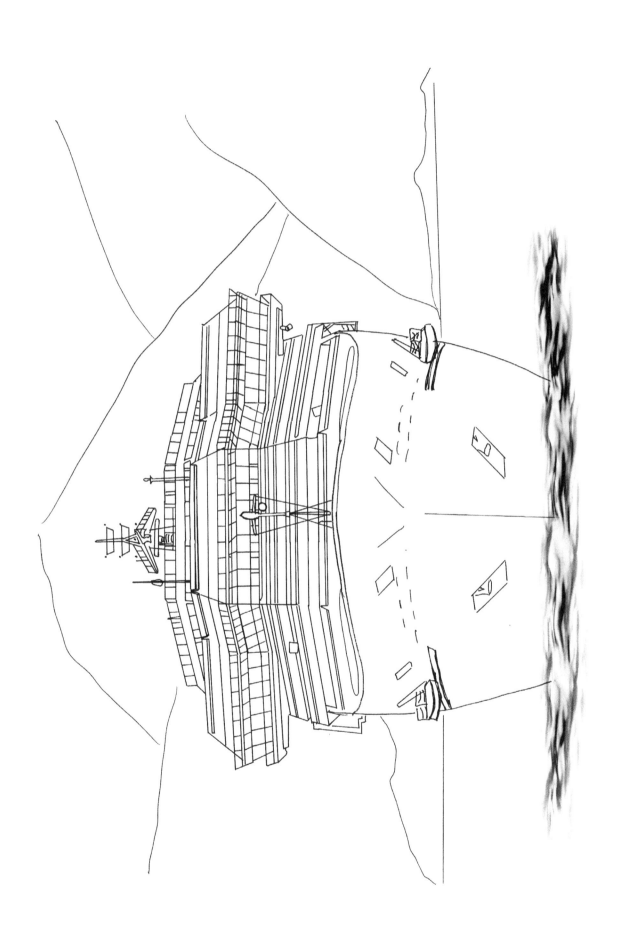

LIBERTY SHIP

The Liberty Ship was a class of cargo ship built in the United States during World War II. Mass-produced on an unprecedented scale, the now iconic Liberty ship came to symbolize U.S. wartime industrial output. The class was built replace ships torpedoed by German U-boats. The vessels were built for the U.S., Britain and the Soviet Union. 2,710 Liberty ships were built in eighteen American shipyards between 1941 and 1945, the largest number of ships ever produced to a single design.

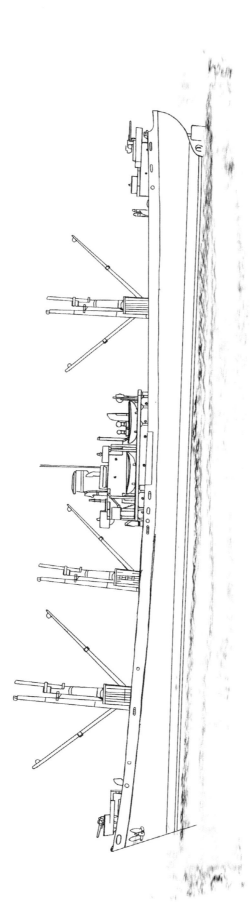

ICEBREAKER

An Icebreaker is a special-purpose ship designed
to navigate through ice and provide
safe waterways for other ships. For a ship to be
considered an icebreaker, it requires three traits that
most normal ships lack: a strengthened hull, an ice-
clearing shape, and the extra power needed to push
through sea ice.
Icebreakers drive their bows onto the ice to break it
using the weight of the ship. Icebreakers also have a
specially designed hull to direct the broken ice around
under or away from the vessel.

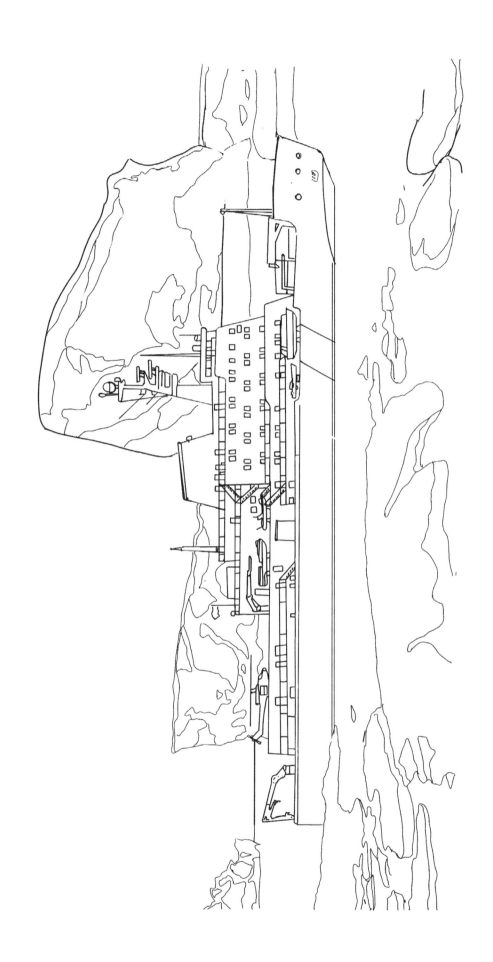

GALLEON

Galleons were the principal warships used by European states from the 16th to 18th centuries during the age of sail.

Galleons generally carried three or more masts with square-rigged sail plans on their fore-mast and main-masts and a lateen fore-and-aft rig on the rear mast. They were generally carvel built with a prominent squared off raised stern.

Such ships were the mainstay of maritime commerce and of the Age of Exploration.

TOUR BOAT

A Tour Boat is used to take tourists on short trips. Tour boats typically start and end in the same place, and normally tour for less than a day. Tour Boats do not usually have accommodations. This contrasts with cruising in large ships for a number of days with accommodation in cabins.

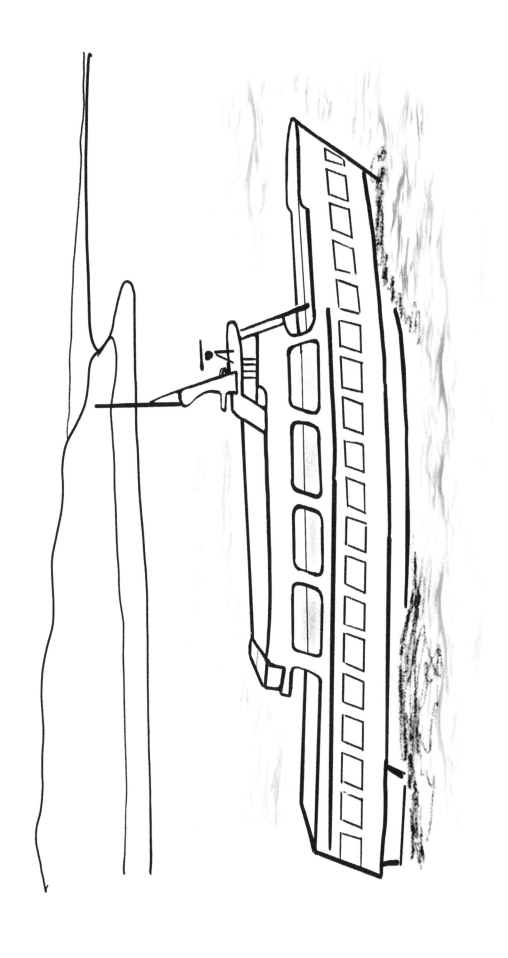

SUBMARINE

Submarines are referred to as boats regardless of their size. They are the only boats capable of independent operation underwater. The term most commonly refers to a large, crewed vessel.

Submarines were first widely used during World War One - (1914–1918), and are now found in many navies. Most large submarines consist of a cylindrical body with hemispherical (or conical) ends and a vertical structure, usually located amidships, which houses communications and sensing devices as well as periscopes. In modern submarines, this structure is the "sail" in American usage, or "fin" in European usage. Conning towers were a feature of earlier designs. They were a separate pressure hull above the main body of the boat that allowed the use of shorter periscopes. Submarines have one of the widest ranges of types and capabilities of any vessel. They range from small autonomous or one- or two-person vessels that operate for a few hours, to large, possibly nuclear powered vessels, that can remain submerged for six months.

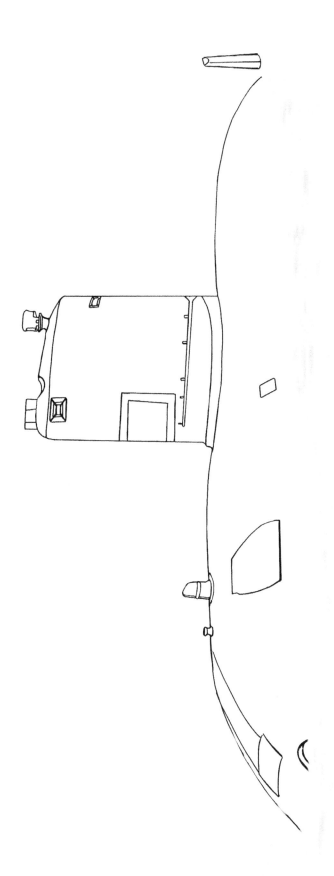

YACHT

A Yacht is a recreational boat. The term originates from the Dutch word *jacht meaning* hunt, and was originally defined as a light fast sailing vessel used by the Dutch navy to pursue pirates around the local shallow waters. In 1660 King Charles II of England used such a vessel to carry him to England and Yacht became a vessel used to convey important persons.

In modern use of the term, yachts are ships or boats used for leisure purposes. There are sailing yachts and power boat yachts.

Yacht lengths normally range from 10 metres (33 ft) up to many meters or hundreds of feet. A luxury craft smaller than 12 metres (39 ft) is more commonly called a cabin cruiser. A superyacht is generally above 24 m (79 ft) and a megayacht is generally over 50 metres (164 ft).

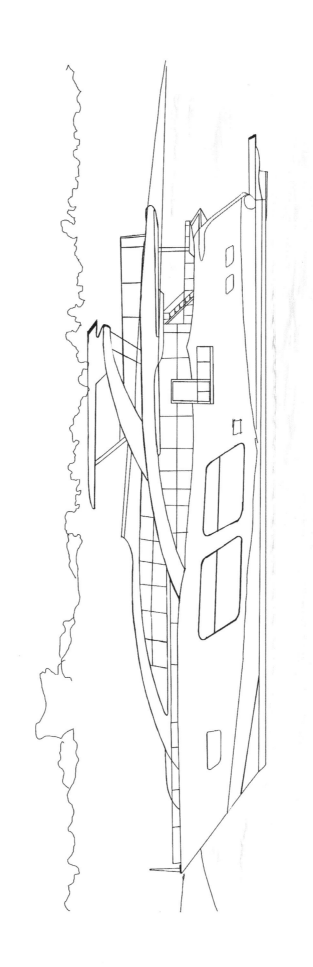

WARSHIP

A Warship is a naval ship that is built and primarily intended for warfare in the open sea or near land. Usually they belong to a country's navy.

As well as being armed, warships are designed to withstand damage and are usually faster and more maneuverable than merchant ships. Unlike a merchant ship, which carries cargo, a warship typically carries only weapons, ammunition and supplies for its crew. Modern warships are generally divided into seven main categories, which are: aircraft-carriers, cruisers, destroyers, frigates, corvettes, submarines and amphibious assault ships.

While many people refer to any warship as a Battleship, actual Battleships were an eighth class. They were very large gun platforms and are not in current service with any navy in the world today.

The warship pictured would represent a Frigate or Destroyer. These ships measure from 130 meters (390 feet) to 160 meters 480 ft in length.

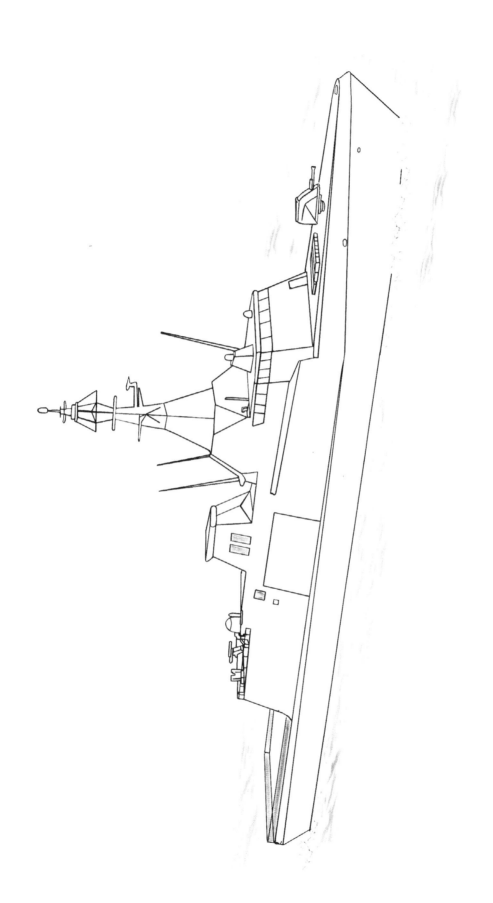

CONTAINER SHIP

Container Ships are cargo ships that carry all of their load in truck-size (intermodal) containers stacked in their holds and on their decks. This technique is called containerization. Container ships carry 90% of seagoing non-bulk cargo today.

Container ship capacity is measured in the number of 20-foot (1-TEU) or 40-foot (2-TEU) standard sized containers. The largest modern container ships can carry over 10,500 - 40 foot containers at one time. Container ships are some of the largest commercial vessels on the ocean rivalling Supertankers.

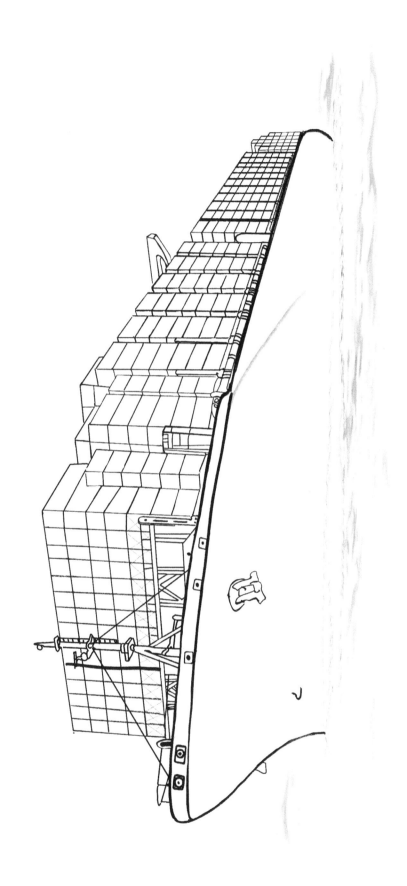

FAST PLATFORM SUPPLY SHIP

A Platform Supply Vessel (PSV) is a ship specially designed to supply offshore oil and gas platforms.   These ships range in length from 50 to 100 meters. The primary function for most of these vessels is logistic support and transportation of goods, tools, equipment and personnel to and from offshore oil platforms and other offshore structures.
Most carry a combination of deck cargoes and bulk cargo, which is stored in tanks below deck, as well as specialty equipment to support firefighting or to assist in oil containment and cleanup of oil spills at sea.

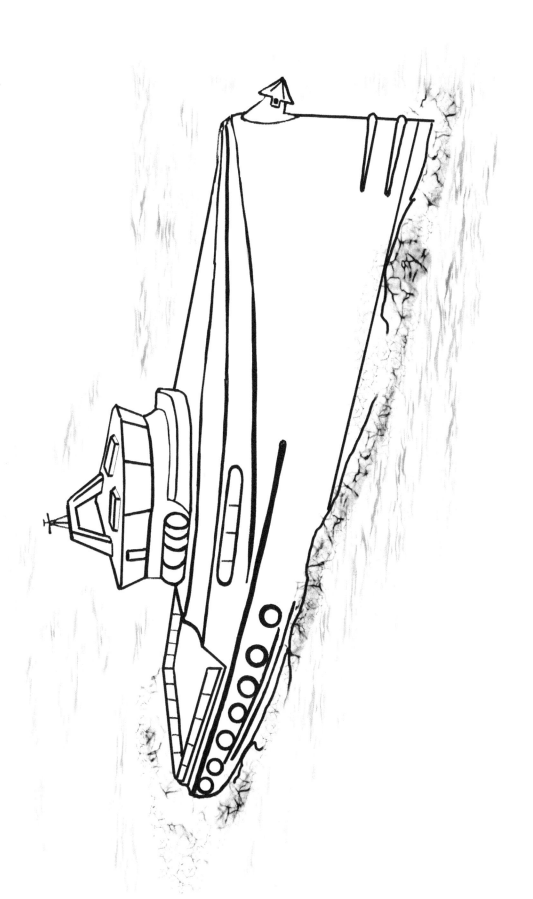

FERRY

A Ferry is a merchant vessel used to carry passengers, vehicles and cargo across a body of water. Most ferries operate regular return services and form a part of the public transport systems of many waterside cities and islands. Ferries allow direct transit between points much like a floating bridge. Ship connections over long distances may also be called ferry services, especially if they carry vehicles.

Types of Ferries include 'Double Ended', 'Hydrofoil', 'Hovercraft', 'Catamaran', 'Roll-on/roll-off', 'Fast RoPax', 'Pontoon', 'Foot Ferries' and 'Cable Ferries'.

The Ferry shown would represent a Fast RoPax Ferry – A conventional ferry with a large garage for cars and large passenger capacity. Fast RoPax ferries sail at over 25 knots (46 km/h; 29 mph).

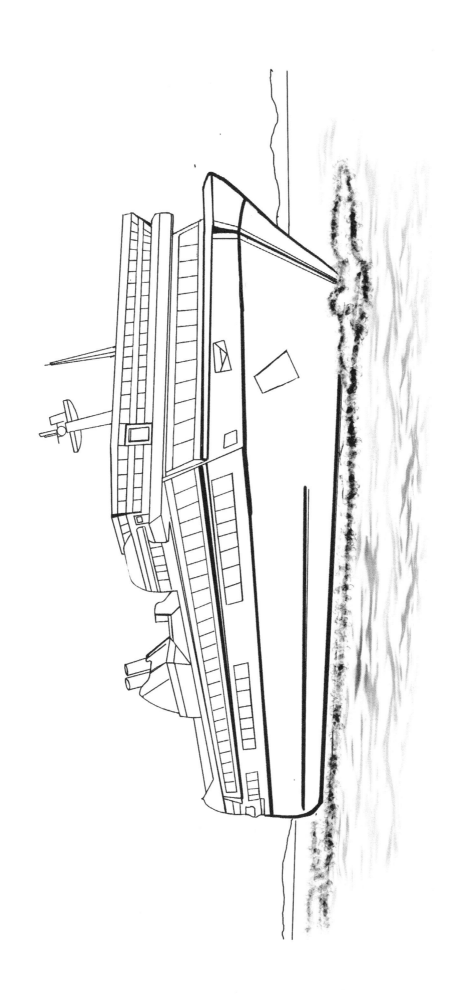

JUNK

A Junk is a type of ancient Chinese sailing ship that is still in use today. Junks were used as seagoing vessels as early as the 2nd century AD and developed rapidly from 960 to 1279. They were originally used throughout Asia. Small numbers are still found, throughout South-East Asia, India, and China. Today there is a growing number of modern recreational junk-rigged sailboats.

The term *junk is* used to cover many kinds of boats but they all employ fully battened sails. The junk's sails make it fast and easily controlled. They include several horizontal stiffeners called "battens", which provide shape and strength. The battens also make the sails more resistant than other sails to large tears, as a tear is typically limited to a single "panel" between battens. The sail-plan of a Junk is spread out between multiple masts, allowing for a comparative powerful sail area,

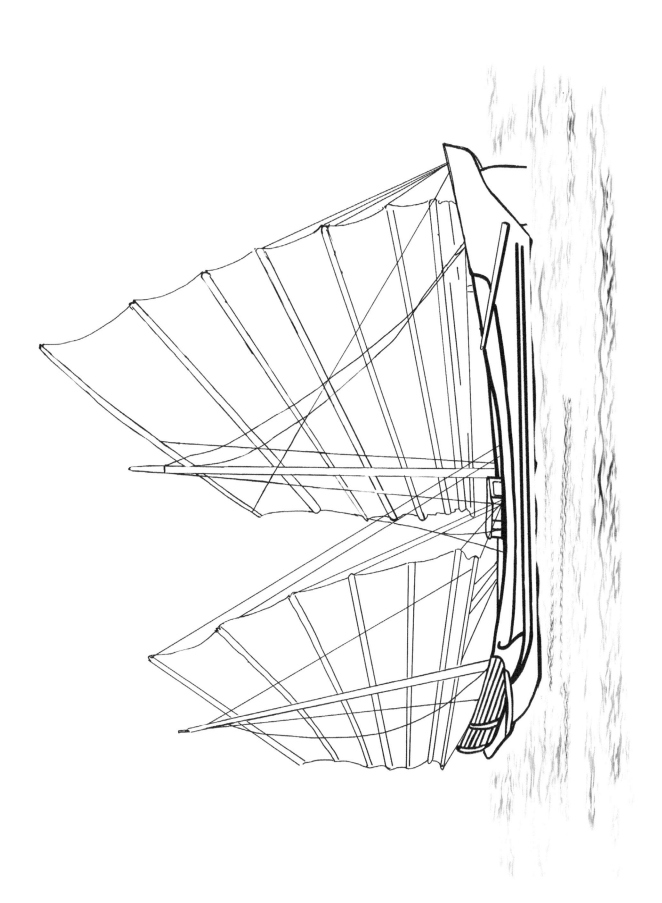

SIDEWHEEL STEAM PACKET

A "Packet Ship" was originally a vessel used to carry mail packets to and from British colonies and outposts. In sea transport today, ships with regular scheduled service that carry freight and passengers are called Packet Ships.

Early steam powered packet ships were powered by paddles. There were two basic ways to mount paddle wheels. Ships with a single wheel on the rear were known as a *sternwheeler*, while those with paddle wheels on each side were known as a *sidewheelers*.

KETCH

A ketch is a sailing craft with two masts. The distinguishing characteristic of a ketch (ketamina) is that the forward of the two masts (the "mainmast") is larger than the after mast (the "mizzen"). To assist going to windward, a ketch may carry one or more jibs or foresails. If a ketch has no jibs, it is called a *cat ketch* or a *periauger* Historically the ketch was a square-rigged vessel, most commonly used as a freighter or fishing boat in the Baltic and North seas. In modern usage, the ketch is a fore-and-aft rigged sailing vessel used as a yacht or pleasure craft.

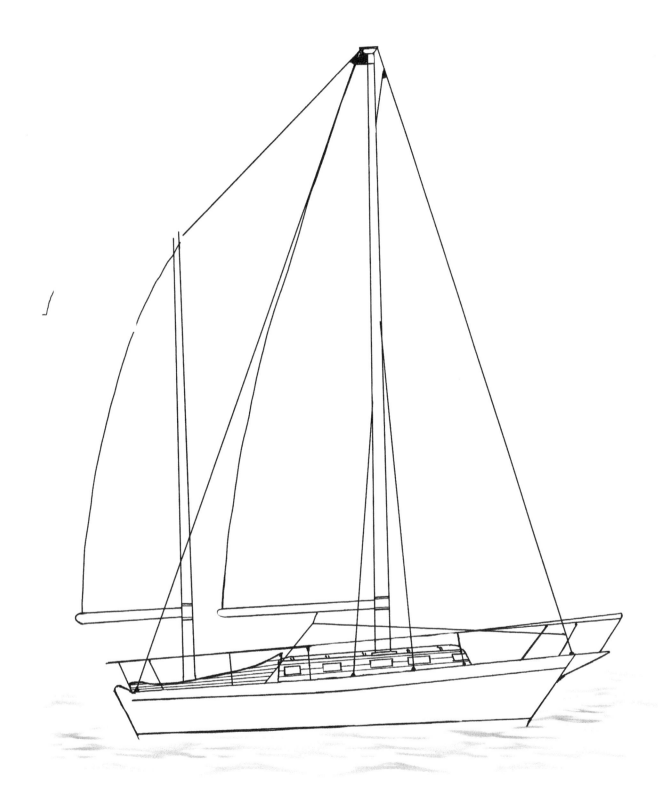

RORO SHIP

Roll-on/roll-off (RORO or ro-ro) Ships are vessels designed to carry cars, trucks, semi-trailers or even railroad cars. Vehicles are driven on and off the ship on their own wheels or are towed using a specialized platform vehicle. RORO vessels usually have built-in ramps that allow the cargo to be efficiently rolled on and off the vessel when in port. While smaller ferries often have built-in ramps, the term RORO is generally reserved for large oceangoing vessels.

Today's pure car carriers (PCC) and their close cousins, the pure car/truck carrier (PCTC), are distinctive ships with a box-like superstructure running the entire length and breadth of the hull. They typically have a stern ramp and a side ramp for dual loading of thousands of vehicles. These kinds of vessels can achieve speeds of more than 19 knots and carry as many as 8,500 cars.

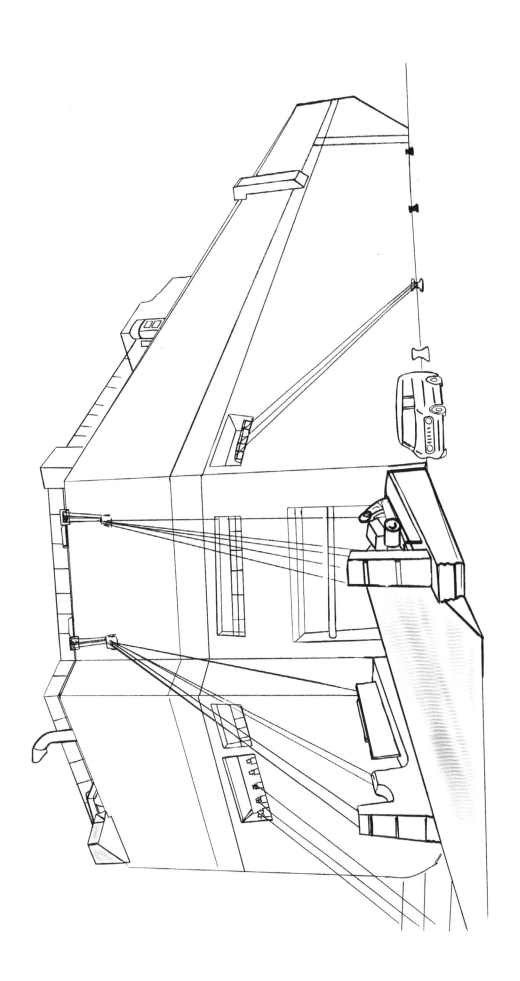

CLASS 1 - OFFSHORE POWERBOAT RACER

Offshore powerboat racing is a type of racing by ocean-going powerboats. This is typically point-to-point racing. The fastest boats are in the Class 1 category, the highest class of offshore powerboat racing. Class 1 is considered one of the most spectacular motorsports in the world. A *Class 1* racing boat has twin-engines and can reach speeds in excess of 257 km/h (160 mph). Boats with two V12 engines are limited to 850 hp at 7600 rpm and boats with V8 engines are limited to 850 hp at 6100 rpm. All boats are limited to a minimum weight of 4950 kg.

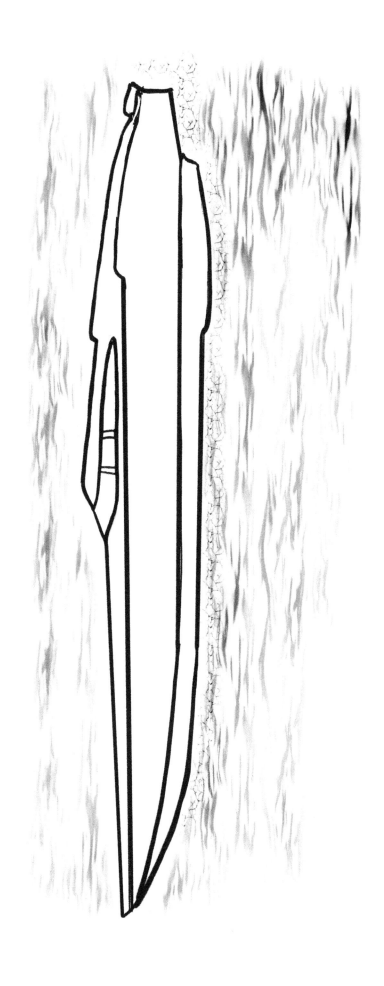

SUPERTANKER

A Supertanker is a very large oil tanker, whose dead-weight capacity exceeds 75,000 tons. The TI ULCC (Ultra Large Crude Carriers) class of supertankers are currently the largest ships in the world. They are too large for the Panama Canal and too large for the Suez Canal except when empty. They can carry 3,166,353 barrels of oil at 16.5 knots (19.0 miles per hour). They are 1,246 feet (380 meters) long, 223 feet (68 meters) wide (beam) and have a draught of 80 ft (24 meters).

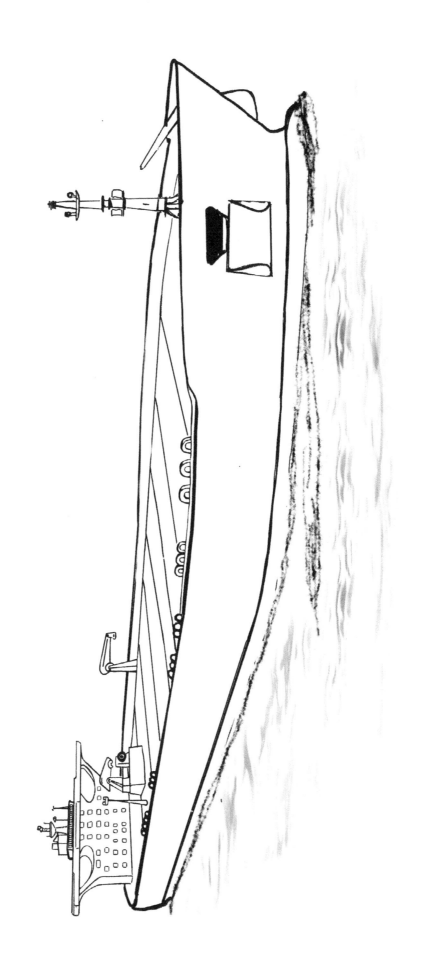

TUGBOAT

A Tugboat or (Tug) is a boat or ship that moves other vessels by pushing or towing them. Tugs move vessels that either should not or cannot move by themselves. They move large ships in crowded harbours, narrow channels or canals. They also push or tow barges, disabled ships, or oil platforms. Tugboats are very powerful for their size. Some Tugboats are built to work in the open ocean. Tugboats sometimes serve as icebreakers, salvage boats or for firefighting, especially in harbors.

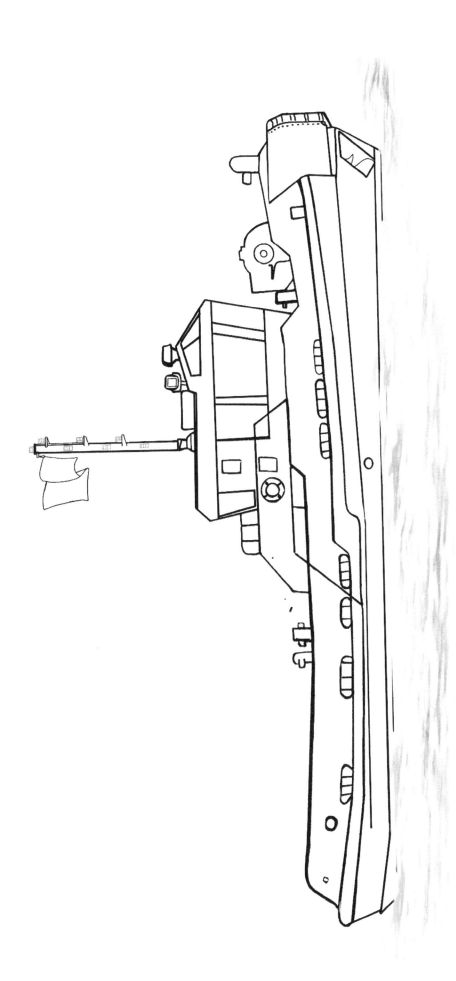

SPACE SHIP – (SPACE PLANE)

Reusable vehicles have been designed only for manned spaceflight, and these are often called spaceplanes. The first partially reusable orbital spacecraft was the Space Shuttle launched by the USA in 1981. During the Shuttle era, six orbiters, five of which have flown in space (*Columbia, Challenger, Discovery, Atlantis,* and *Endeavour. Challenger* was lost in January 1986 and *Columbia* in February 2003.

The Space Shuttles were retired in 2011. The Shuttle's human transport role is to be replaced by Space X's Dragon V2 and Boeing's CST-100 Starliner. The Shuttle's heavy cargo transport role is to be replaced by expendable rockets.

Many organizations are working on Space Plans or Space Ships that will carry tourists or space travellers in the future. Humans will one day travel to other planets in Space Ships, the same way early Europeans sailed to new lands in Sailing Ships.

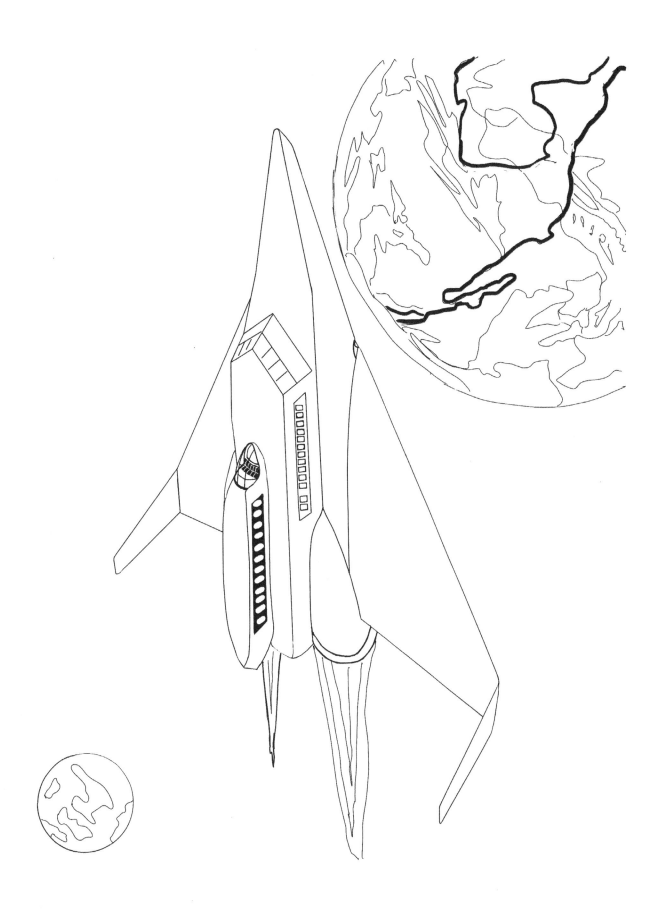

Made in the USA
Las Vegas, NV
05 August 2021